To commemorate the
life and achievements of

Ian Simon Wadsworth

1965 - 1997

Registered Osteopath

- ❖ MSc Sports Medicine
- ❖ BSc Osteopathy
- ❖ Paramedic
- ❖ R.G.N.

This book has been kindly donated
by the family of the above, to ensure
that future generations of osteopathic
students receive the same excellent
training that he himself had

**Other martial arts books
available from A & C Black**

INJURY·FREE
KARATE

**This book is to be returned on or before
the last date stamped below.**

CONTENTS

First published 1992 by
A & C Black (Publishers) Limited
35 Bedford Row, London WC1R 4JH

ISBN 0 7136 3573 8

A CIP catalogue record for this book
is available from the British Library.

Printed and bound in Great Britain by
Whitstable Litho Ltd, Whitstable, Kent

ACKNOWLEDGEMENTS

I would like to thank Mr Barry Shearer, head instructor of Enfield Dojo and London Area Officer for Jin Sei Kai, for his help in demonstrating correct and incorrect techniques for the photographs in this book. I would also like to thank Mr Tom Hill, head instructor of Grovehill Dojo (Jin Sei Kai), for performing some of the techniques in his shorts so that things can be seen more clearly.

Special thanks are due to Mrs Wendy Russell of Watford Dojo (Jin Sei Kai), who volunteered to distort her body in a leotard so that we could clearly show what happens when a joint is hyperextended. Wendy is a particularly good subject for this, as her elbow joint has a large articulation of movement. She is, in fact, a very competent karateka and never actually hyperextends any of her joints during a proper training session!

I would also like to thank Miss Sue Pine of Sizewell Dojo (Jin Sei Kai) for the many long hours she has spent in front of a word processor helping me to put this book together.

Finally, my thanks to Cameron Angus (Grad. Dip. (Phys)., M.C.S.P., S.R.P.), chartered physiotherapist, for all his help with the anatomy, physiology and injury prevention information contained within the text.

Kanazawa Sensei with author Paul Perry
at the Jin Sei Kai Honbu Dojo

FOREWORD

Mr Paul Perry is publishing a book about training and progressing in karate without damaging joints and muscles. I am convinced that the contents of this book will be very valuable. I am most proud of Mr Perry, as he is one of the best karate instructors amongst my tens of thousands of students.

About 4000 years ago in China, Karate-do originated as a medical exercise called Kung-fu. It then developed into the Chinese Kenpo. Later on, it became the modern Karate-do by adopting and using Okinawan martial arts and Japanese traditional culture of the martial arts spirits. Therefore the use of karate is:

- exercise for infants
- physical exercise for children
- sports for youngsters
- discipline and self-defence
- keep fit for women and the elderly
- rehabilitation for those with disabilities.

So, karate has a wide-ranging capacity to conform to modern society.

Mr Paul Perry has a good knowledge of Karate-do history and I am very pleased that he is introducing his results of scientific research to karateka all over the world. I strongly recommend this book to everybody.

Shotokan Karate International

President   HIROKAZU KANAZAWA

Paul Perry executing tobi yoko geri to B. Shearer

ABOUT THE AUTHOR

Paul Perry is an EKC, EKGB and WUKO recognised 6th Dan. He is the Chief Instructor of Jin Sei Kai Kanazawa Ryu. The name 'Jin Sei Kai' was given to him by Kanazawa Sensei and means 'Human Life Association', but it also has many other meanings about life. The association was formed in 1977 within Shotokan Karate International. In 1985, JSK left the SKI and became an independent body.

Mr Perry has trained in Shotokan Karate for the last twenty-five years, studying under the guidance of Kanazawa Sensei for the large majority of that time. He has also trained under most of the top Japanese Shotokan exponents and many of the high ranking Tai Chi Chuan masters during his travels to Japan and other Far Eastern countries. He now practises and teaches Tai Chi. Paul is a former member of the international squad for Shotokan Karate International, representing Great Britain in kata and kumite, and was also the London and Home Counties Area Officer and Grading Examiner for the SKI. In 1981-2 he received the Wilkinson Sword of Honour for achievements in karate. As a senior self defence coach with the Martial Arts Commission, he was a member of the Coaching and Technical Committees of the now disbanded English Karate Council, and he is now a member of both the Coaching and Technical Committees of the new governing body, English Karate Great Britain. He holds regular advanced training sessions for Jin Sei Kai and visiting instructors at the Honbu Dojo in Watford. He still travels worldwide, teaching and gathering any knowledge which could be integrated into bettering karate training.

INTRODUCTION

The reason I decided to write a book with a slightly more detailed look at basic techniques than is found in many other karate books is that over the past twenty-five years I have seen a large number of needless injuries occurring as a result of bad training practice. People from various styles have spoken to me about the physical problems they suffer, mostly connected with their joints, many of which should not have taken place if they had had a little more understanding about the movements they were trying to achieve. Also, many karateka often listen to what a particular teacher is saying but misunderstand what the teacher is trying to put across.

In my opinion, I have been very fortunate to have studied under Kanazawa Sensei for twenty years. His teaching during that time has looked closely at the finer points of Shotokan techniques. Sensei and myself have sat for many hours in my home during his trips to England and have discussed the finer points of karate and how misunderstandings have been widespread. We have also discussed the great importance of how to use the breath and the internal organs – but this would perhaps require another book! When we ran large courses, he often used to tell the students that eighty per cent of karate practice is devoted to promoting health and only twenty per cent is for self defence. If you analyse this, it is perfectly true: most people who do Budo karate seldom use the defence side, but the benefits of training properly enhance their daily lives.

For many years I was the South of England Grading Examiner for Shotokan Karate International and this enabled me to visit many dojos. In the early days I found that a lot of misunderstandings had occurred because of the language differences between Japanese and English and because of the interpretation of the instructions given to the people running dojos by visiting Japanese instructors. As I travel round the country today, visiting dojos where I am invited to teach, even after all these years of karate being practised in Europe, I still see students using their bodies in ways which can and do end up in debilitating injuries, even when they are performing static techniques which do not involve fast movement. With a little more knowledge of how the body works and what one hopes to achieve from the outcome of a technique, these injuries can be avoided as far as basic movement is concerned.

When I am asked to teach, I try to teach karate rather than just to instruct the class to move up and down the dojo doing various techniques. Once a student understands what he should be trying to achieve by the techniques, it often requires many hours of dedication and practising that technique over and over again before it can be done well. This can be overseen by the club instructors after I have gone, so during my training sessions we analyse some of the techniques of kihon, kata or kumite. With a little more thought and feeling than may have been shown in earlier sessions, we get a far more enjoyable result and a much less injurious one.

Most karateka hope to keep on training for many years. However, if a joint is moved badly for years on end and adverse pressure is placed upon it, the ultimate consequence will probably be the failure of that joint to function correctly. This, in my opinion, is not the aim of practising karate.

In my association, Jin Sei Kai, I hold regular classes for instructors so that they can analyse and understand the movements that they are teaching and therefore ensure they are instructing other people properly. I see this as being most important because instructors, or anyone else teaching karate, are responsible for the physical health of the people coming into their care to learn karate.

We have newer and more modern information available these days than when I started training twenty-five years ago, but the legacy of misunderstanding caused in the early days by language barriers still lives on. Many European instructors have taken too literally the meaning of certain movements. A good example is the instruction to keep the back leg straight. The back leg should be 'straight', as we will discuss later in the book, but it is held straight by the muscle groups and not hyperextended against the knee, which could damage and weaken the knee joint. We must also take into consideration that if a European is doing karate (or, in fact, many Eastern people nowadays) he will be taller in stature than were many of our Eastern forefathers. Therefore, he needs to look at the different leverages that the extra length in his limbs can produce.

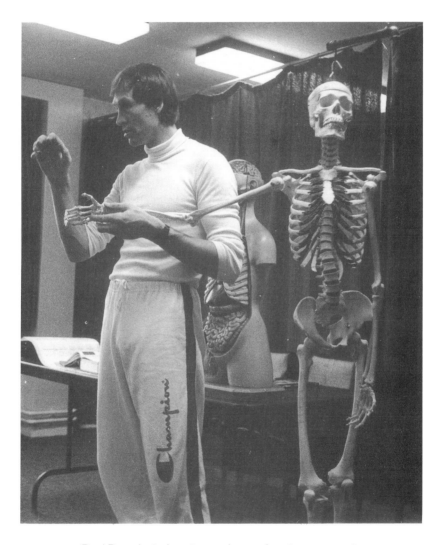

Paul Perry lecturing at a seminar on karate movement

If karate is done properly, we generate and place upon the body an enormous amount of energy and stress, so it is imperative that we try to minimise any misunderstanding of basic movements. These are the foundation stones for all, or most of, the other movements. It is also very difficult and takes a great deal of willpower and dedication in training to change the way we move our bodies if we have interpreted the movement incorrectly in the beginning of our karate life.

Even if you are training correctly, with everything done as close to perfection as possible, with the best will in the world, continual fast movement and the amount of pressures that are put on the body will result in fatigue and an impairment of technical ability. This is the time to stop and relax with some breathing exercises if you are trying to achieve a better technical understanding. So, remember that fatigue can play a large part in executing techniques badly.

The movements shown in this book are the basic techniques learned by Shotokan karateka. However, to a certain extent, style is irrelevant here, because most martial artists use punches, kicks, strikes, etc. and may also find some interesting and useful information. It is my hope that the information will enable students and instructors alike to gain a little bit more from their art or teaching. My sole aim in writing this book is that people can enjoy their style properly without suffering for it in years to come.

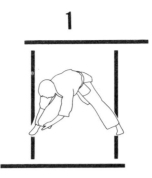

1

COMMON FAULTS IN THE WARM-UP

In karate, and in Shotokan in particular, we tend to use a warm-up which is loosely based on a Buddhist yoga warm-up sequence. I shall not go into too much detail on warm-ups and stretching here, as there are many good books available on various ways of warming the body and stretching using PNF and other plyometric exercises which can be integrated into the warm-up session. I am therefore just mentioning a few exercises which can give trouble if care is not taken before all the technical parts of karate training begin. You should, however, not take warm-ups and body toning and conditioning lightly, since they constitute a very important and integral part of the whole of karate training.

NECK
The correct way to stretch the neck muscles is to stretch the head forwards and backwards (as in photographs 1 and 1a) and then to

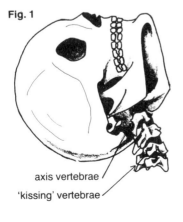

Fig. 1

Fig. 1 Axis vertebrae being ground away by neck rolls

axis vertebrae

'kissing' vertebrae

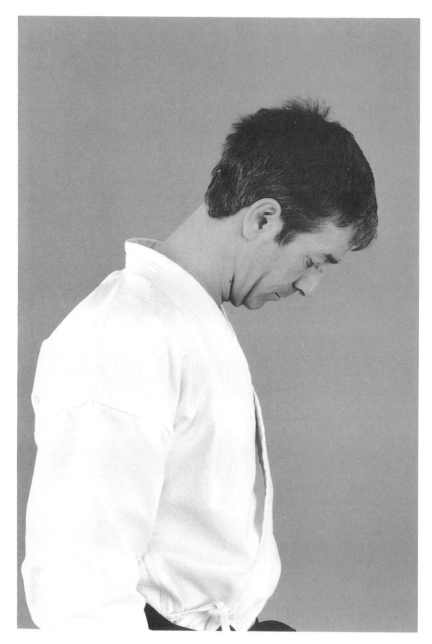

1 Head forwards

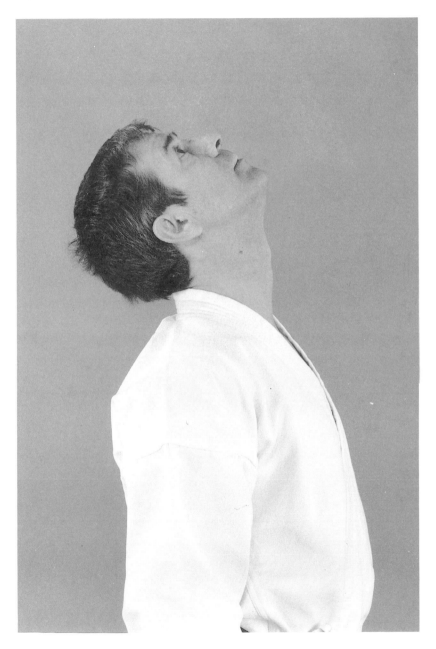

1a Head back

twist the head from side to side (as in photographs 2 and 2a). Then relax the head over towards the shoulder as far as possible without strain (as in photographs 3 and 3a). Avoid complete neck rolls. Over a period of time they grind down the axis vertebrae in the neck, causing serious problems at the top of the spine.

2 Head to the left

2a   Head to the right

3 Ear to the left shoulder

3a Ear to the right shoulder

ARMS

When warming up arms and shoulders be careful not to throw the arms back behind the body with a violent action (as in photograph 4). This is the first thing many people do when warming the shoulders and chest area, but this can cause tearing in the pectoral muscles and can weaken the ligaments around the shoulder joints.

4 Do not throw the arms back with force,
because this could tear the pectoral muscles

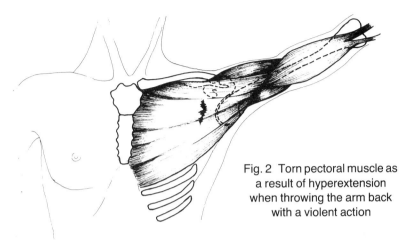

Fig. 2 Torn pectoral muscle as
a result of hyperextension
when throwing the arm back
with a violent action

It is best to take care and warm the arms up slowly, using circular motions. In general, when warming up the arms sudden stretches should be avoided. Gentle stretching is better, followed by static stretching. PNF (proprioceptive neuromuscular facilitation – 'contract-relax') is also very good.

HIPS

In all hip exercises, keep the weight of the hips over the feet if possible. This puts less strain on the lumbar region.

KNEES

The ligaments around the knees are best warmed up by a circular motion of the knees. Keep the knees locked in a slightly bent position and circle from the hips and ankles. Knee bounces are all right as long as they are not overextended and the joint is controlled. Never do bunny hops.

BACK STRETCHES

In stretching the back and hamstrings, never try to force the body to go beyond its natural limits. Never stretch down, breathe out and try to stretch down further. If, as in photograph 5, you stand with your feet apart and try to stretch your head towards your right

5 Gently stretching towards the right knee

knee, you should not hold the right leg and yank your body down towards that knee, as this only forces the muscles to shorten themselves. It is better to go as far as you can and hold the position for roughly six seconds (as in photograph 5a). This will give a greater flexibility to the body than jerking, as I have previously mentioned. Prior to this, gentle ballistic stretching, in my opinion, is fine as long as it is done within the body's natural limits. In any exercise which involves twisting the spine, keep your back straight.

5a Holding the stretch for greater flexibility

HURDLER STRETCH

(See photograph 6.) Begin the hurdler stretch by sitting on the floor and drawing the ankle of the leg you are going to fold behind up to your hip. Then fold the leg behind you, keeping the ankle tight against your buttock. When leaning forwards (as in photograph 6a), only go as far as your body will allow you to go. The first indication of overstretching occurs when the hip of the leg that is being stretched starts to lift off the floor; the hamstring of that leg

6 Hurdler stretch

6a Hurdler stretch – stretching forwards.
Hold the position, but do not overstretch

6b Hurdler stretch – leaning forwards between the knees.
Do not allow the buttocks to lift off the ground,
as this will strain the knee ligaments

6c Going against the joint of the right leg. Hold the position for six seconds, but
without overstretching

will start pulling quite dramatically, so you know you are over-
straining your body. At this point you are putting the medial ligament of the leg that is folded behind under great strain.

Also, when leaning the body forwards but equally between the
outstretched leg and the folded back leg (as in photograph 6b), and
also when going against the joint of the leg that is folded back (as in
photograph 6c), never allow the hip of the extended leg to lift from

the floor. If this happens, the medial ligament will again come under an enormous amount of pressure. As with the back and hamstring stretches, it is far better to go as far as one can and just try to relax and hold the position for about fifteen to twenty seconds, perhaps repeating the exercise several times.

SITTING BACK BETWEEN THE LEGS

Sitting back between the legs should be done with extreme caution (see photograph 7) and only if you have enough flexibility in the hips to allow you to sit on the floor completely; otherwise, this could cause damage by overstretching the medial ligaments of both knees. Unless you are supple enough in the upper hips to allow a good rotation of the leg, it may be better to avoid this exercise.

7 Only do this exercise if you can actually sit on the floor, otherwise it will strain rather than stretch the body

LEG SWINGS

Trying to swing the leg too high when doing leg swings can tear the hamstrings. To avoid this, push the hips forward. Point the toes to

8 Leg swings. Warming up prior to fast techniques. Start with the toes down to ease tension in the back of the legs

start with, as this will ease the tension in the back of the leg (see photograph 8), but don't swing the leg higher than is comfortable without strain, as this can also destabilise the knee of the supporting leg and cause problems to the ligaments in this area. After three or four relaxed swings, you can gently swing the leg up with the toes pulled back (as in photograph 8a).

8a Leg swings with the foot back. Only do this after you have followed the advice for photograph 8

2

PUNCHES

CHOKU TZUKI (chudan)

This is one of the first techniques that is taught in Jin Sei Kai. It is important to teach all the various points outlined below correctly and to understand the faults, as many of them are common to other punches and strikes and utilise the same joint and muscle systems.

Stand with the feet hip-width apart facing forwards and parallel (see photograph 9). The knees should be slightly bent. Extend the

9 Yoi

33

9a Start position for choku tzuki

left hand in line with the sternum, with the wrist bent so that the fingers point upwards and the little finger faces forwards (see photograph 9a). The right fist should be drawn back over the right hip, with the elbow tucked in and the wrist straight.

9b Half-way position for choku tzuki

Pull the left hand (forming a fist) back towards the hip and simultaneously propel the right hand out. At the half-way point both elbows should brush against the rib cage so that the fists move in a straight line (see photograph 9b). The arms should work together

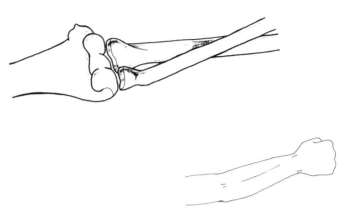

Fig. 3 Correct elbow joint in gyaku tzuki

with an equal and opposite action. This economy of movement gives the body greater stability as far as balance is concerned.

When the right elbow leaves the rib cage and starts to move forwards, the elbow should be rotated (see fig. 3), causing it to move slightly outwards from the line of attack. At the point of focus, pull the shoulders down and lock the arm out with the muscles of the arm and shoulder. If the elbow has been correctly rotated a very slight bend should remain in the arm, with a few centimetres of movement left by the time focus is reached (see photograph 9c).

On no account should the arm be locked straight, with bone against bone. The first two knuckles of the punching fist should be in line with the sternum. The wrist should be straight and not cocked up or down. The little finger should be tightly rolled in order to tense the tendon on the outside of the arm. At the point of kimae, breathe out. Push the head and chest (4th dorsal vertebrae) up at the same time. The hip of the punching side moves slightly forwards and the muscles of the hip, buttock and stomach should simultaneously lock as hard as possible. The body should have complete muscular connection throughout at the point of focus. After a period of constant practice, this should produce a vibration throughout the body. If a jarring sensation occurs, the muscles are not all being tensed in the correct unison. This jarring can cause stress to various parts of the body, particularly the shoulders, chest and spine.

9c Choku tzuki completed, with the arm straight but not hyperextended

Points to watch

The rotation of the elbow is most important. It loosens the shoulder and allows the fist and the whole of the lower arm to turn through 180 degrees and to be locked in place with the muscles of the shoulder and the upper arm. Simply rotating the wrist alone does not allow all the muscle groups to lock in and the elbow tends to hyperextend. At the beginning of the punch the elbow must not move out and away from the body (see photograph 10). If this does happen, the elbow, having gone through its half rotational movement, is snapped straight as it completes the punch (photograph 10a).

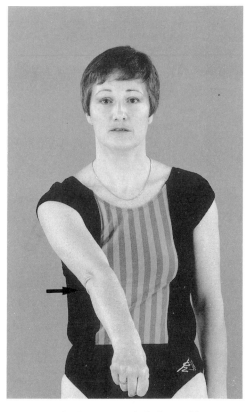

10 Poorly executed choku tzuki – half-way stage. Elbows are leaving the side of the body

10a Badly executed choku tzuki, showing hyperextended elbow

Fig. 4 Incorrect choku tzuki (right elbow, viewed from above), showing hyperextension of the elbow and consequent ramming of the ulna against the humerus, and tearing of the biceps tendon

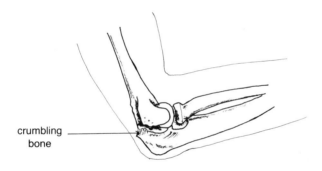

crumbling bone

Fig. 5 An ulna crumbling against the radius

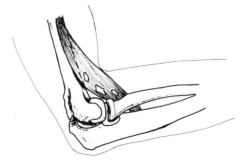

Fig. 6 Build-up of bony matter in soft tissue in the elbow region, caused by misuse of the elbow in punching

In the short term this can cause hyperextension and consequent damage to the protective sleeve of the joint capsule and over-stretching of the biceps tendon. The long-term consequences are far more serious. The jarring action of the ulna jamming against the radius can lead to trauma of the inside of the joint because of the sudden violent movement. If this happens repeatedly, wear and tear can set in well before its time and predispose the student to arthritis. The glistening smooth surface of the inside of the bone starts to corrugate and eventually to fissure, leading to pressure on the nerve endings, pain and swelling. The elbow reacts very badly to violent tugging movements like this, which in some cases can cause a build-up of bone in the muscle tissue itself.

GYAKU TZUKI (right hand)

From geden barai, gyaku tzuki should be performed as follows. The left hand should be raised in a similar position to the start of choku tzuki, i.e. in line with the sternum (see photograph 11) and the head and eyes forward. The right elbow should be pulled back tightly and the shoulders kept down in a similar position to choku tzuki, except that the body should now be hanmi (half-facing). The chin should be relaxed and kept in, not sticking forwards, as this can make a difference to the control factor as you punch. Keep the back straight and relaxed and the hips at a 45 degree angle (it is not necessary to draw the hips back further than this), making sure that from the hip width position the body is maintained within the extremities of the foot position. Keep the front knee bent; the big toe should be turned one toe's distance (maximum) inside towards the centre line of the body. The rear knee should be twisted out as much as possible, which puts pressure on the rear foot and helps to keep it flat as long as the rear foot is at a 45 degree angle (see photograph 11 again).

When executing gyaku tzuki, the actual punch is basically the same as choku tzuki, except that the gyaku tzuki has the propulsion of the hips and the spring-loading of the rear leg against the floor adding force and momentum to it.

As the punch is executed, the front arm is drawn back and the rear arm simultaneously moves forwards until both elbows are

11   Gyaku tzuki – yoi position

squeezing the lower ribs (photograph 11a). At this point, slightly relax the rear leg and hip. Then twist the hip and rotate the whole of the rear leg, so that the knee has rotated through a quarter circle towards the ground. The foot should remain still. Push the right hip forwards as far as possible, but keep the left hip relaxed, drawn down and slightly back. The front knee will move slightly forwards at this stage but do not let it move out to the left. The inner thigh

11a Gyaku tzuki – half-way position. Note: hips are still in the original hanmi position and the elbows are touching the body

muscles are then locked as the right arm is fully extended, with a half rotation of the elbow, and the left hand is pulled back.

As in choku tzuki, the stomach, buttocks and whole body should simultaneously be focused. It is better to allow the whole body to move slightly forwards rather than trying to counteract this by taking the shoulders and the body back, since this could have a detrimental effect on the lumbar region.

11b Completed gyaku tzuki

At the point of kimae there should be a vibrational effect, not a jarring sensation, throughout the body. The muscles of the hip and leg should be relaxed slightly and then twisted forwards and kimaed without any compacting of the joints. Also, you should neither hyperextend the joint nor push against it.

In a correct gyaku tzuki, the rear knee is rolled in so that the hips, facing forwards, are locked against each other and the student has full use of all the muscle groups. Beginners often fail to lock in the hips and try to push in to the punch by overextending the back, which puts a great strain on the lumbar region.

Points to avoid

From the starting position with the left hand forward, many people have the front toe straight in line and, although the feet are hip width apart, the rear foot is sticking out at a 90 degree angle (see photographs 12 and 12a). The leg is locked straight and the hip is

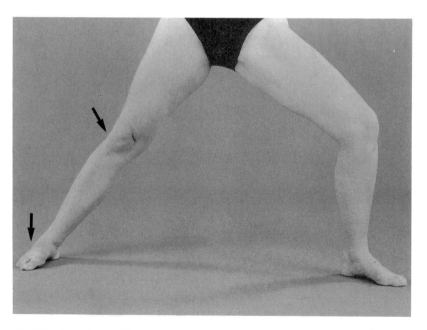

12 Side view of unstable zenkutsu dachu. Note the rear foot at the wrong angle and the leg too straight, causing the knee joint cavity to open on the inside

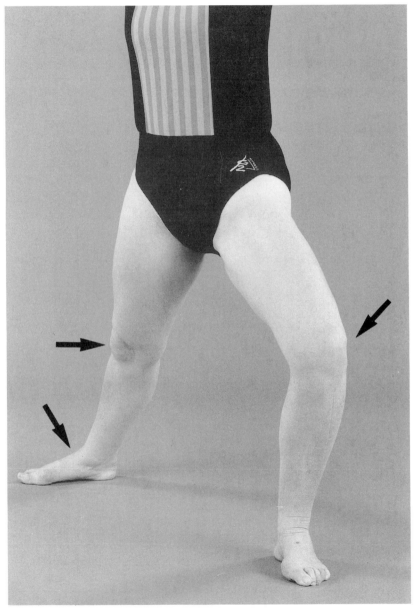

12a Front view of zenkutsu dachu, again showing rear foot, rear knee and front knee all in bad positions. This makes for a totally unstable stance

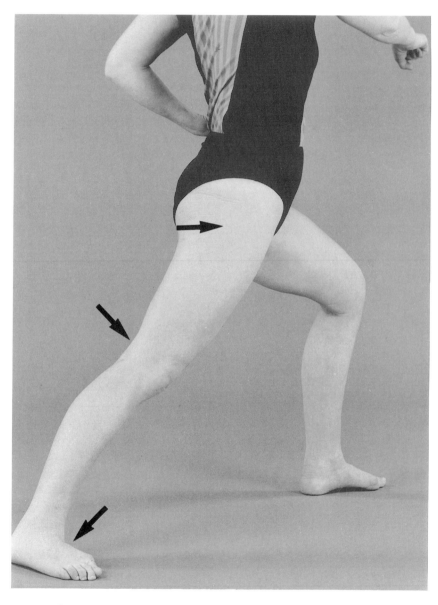

13 Gyaku tzuki – bad foot placement and hyperextended rear leg, which prevents the hips from functioning correctly. It also has a straining and grinding effect on the rear knee joint

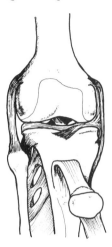 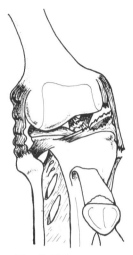 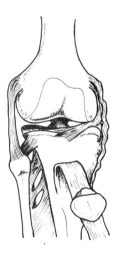

Fig. 7 Normal right knee, with equal pressure on both sides

Fig. 8 Extreme wear of right knee, leading to tearing of the anterior cruciate cartilage and the medial colateral cartilage

Fig. 9 Right knee – the cavity is open on the lateral side

drawn back too far, being completely side-on, which makes the front knee move inwards. As the punch moves through and the hip is rotated forwards, the upper part of the body pulls the upper rear leg round (photograph 13). This strains the medial ligament and results eventually in swelling and chronic pain caused by many tiny tears inside the ligament. In serious cases the medial ligament tears completely, followed by the tearing of the anterior cruciate inside the knee. The medial cartilage might then also rip.

The back, too, is an area of potential danger if this move is not performed correctly. Many people push the shoulders back and draw the hips and coccyx up towards the shoulders, pushing out the belly and chest and causing the spine to bow forwards (photograph 14). This can cause the spinous processes (the bony parts of the spine that you can feel sticking out on your back) to knock together with a 'kissing' action, resulting in inflammation and backache. Hyperextension of the lumbar region can strain the powerful psoas muscle that runs from the spine to the front of the leg, causing it to go into painful spasm.

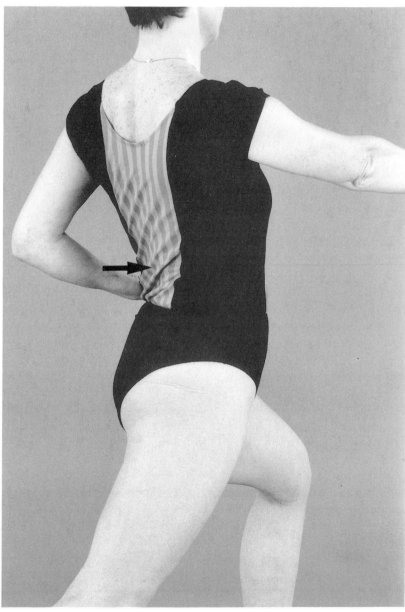

14 Gyaku tzuki performed with an excessively bowed spine, causing a 'kissing' action of the vertebrae

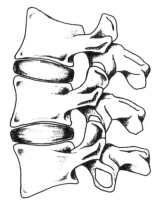
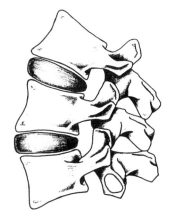

Fig. 10 Normal spine   Fig. 11 'Kissing' spine

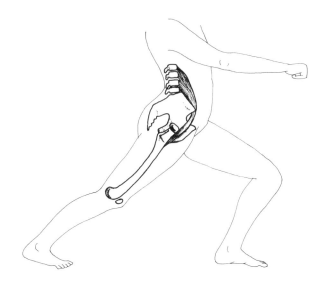

Fig. 12 Strain on the psoas muscle, which causes back pain,
especially in women in later life

Locking the joints of the knee and elbow is most detrimental
both to the joints themselves and to the ligaments around them.

STANCES

ZENKUTSU DACHU

The front foot should point straight ahead with a very slight turn (one toe's width) towards the centre. The rear foot should also point as far as possible in the direction you are going – at least 45 degrees if you can get it. The feet should be hip distance apart.

15 Correct zenkutsu dachu

When the hips are at 45 degrees to the direction of travel, as in gedan barai, the rear knee should be flexed outwards. When the hips are at 90 degrees, as in gyaku tzuki, the rear knee should be rolled in. This section protects the knee ligaments from strain and long-term wear.

A bad zenkutsu dachu can cause a great deal of damage to the knee joints. The rear knee should never ever be locked out straight, because this puts undue pressure on the cartilage and medial ligaments. You should also try to keep the rear foot flat (as in photograph 15) whilst performing basic techniques and not allow the outside edge of the foot to roll up (as in photograph 16), as this destabilises the stance and causes unnecessary strain in exactly the same way as explained in the 'Points to avoid' section in gyaku tzuki. Using a left zenkutsu dachu (front stance) the rear right leg and left front leg can be damaged. The front knee is forced out sideways, which puts strain on the ligaments there. Instead, lock the rear leg out with the thigh muscles, leaving a very slight bend in the knee.

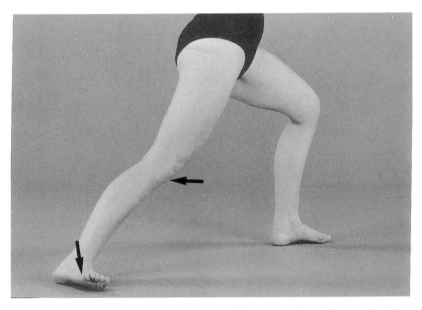

16 Zenkutsu dachu – bad foot placement. The outer edge of the rear foot is rolling up, causing excessive pressure to the inside of the knee joint

KOKUTSU DACHU

In a good back stance the hips should be at 45 degrees to the direction of travel and both hips should be kept as soft as possible. The rear foot should be at 90 degrees to the front one and the rear knee should be out over the toe. The centre line of the front knee should be in line with the front foot (see photographs 17 and 17a).

17 Back stance – side on, showing correct foot placement, and hip and knee positioning

17a Shuto uke (knife-hand block), showing correct foot positioning and correct hip angles to give power to the front striking arm

Points to avoid

The front knee should never be allowed to drop in because this places pressure on the medial ligaments (see photograph 18) and causes damage to them. The quadraceps around the inside of the joint can weaken. If the rear knee is allowed to drop in (as in photo-

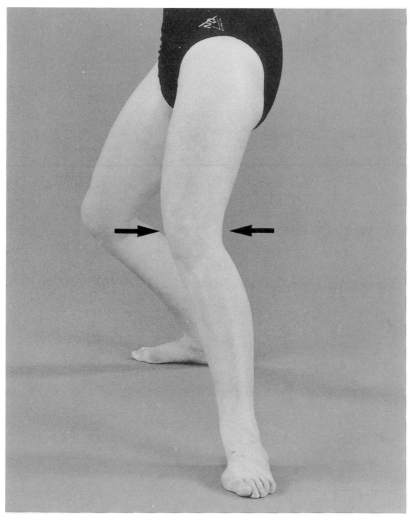

18 Back stance viewed from the front. If the front knee is allowed to drop to the inside of the stance, excessive pressure will be put on the knee joint

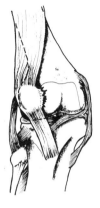

Fig. 13 Right knee (support leg), as in photograph 19, showing dislocation of the patella. This is especially likely to happen if the foot should slip on perspiration

graph 19), the kneecap is pulled back onto the joint at an angle rather than being pulled back straight, thus straining and grinding onto the joint, especially if the joint is spending a lot of time flexed.

Anterior knee pain can also develop between the kneecap and the femur because of the stress transmitted to it. The medial ligament is again at risk, as previously mentioned in the section on gyaku tzuki. If the hips are turned too much to the side (see also photographs 18 and 19), the front knee tends to lock, which can also damage the joints. Stiffness in the rear hip and a badly positioned rear foot not only make the stance unstable, but they wreck the joints. A lot of knee damage can be prevented by keeping the rear knee pushed out. This in turn makes the ankles more supple over a period of time.

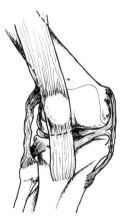

Fig. 14 Left knee (front knee in this stance), showing the patella being strained as a result of the hips being drawn round too far

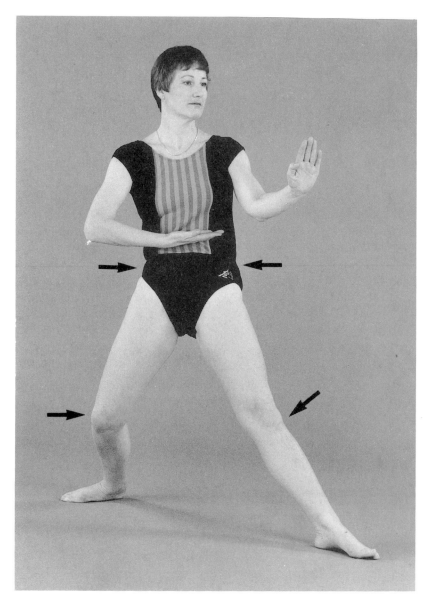

19 Bad shuto uke, showing poor leg positioning. The rear knee has been allowed to drop to the inside of the stance, which could cause kneecap damage. The front hips are badly positioned and the stance is therefore very unstable

20 Poorly executed knife-hand block, showing too much forward movement before rocking back into kokutsu dachu

When performing movements in backstance, such as blocks like shuto uchi, you should move smoothly through from one position to the next. Many people, especially when moving forwards, tend to start the block in more of a zenkutsu dachu position (as in photograph 20) and then rock back into a kokutsu dachu stance. This often results in the backside sticking out past the line of the feet (as in photograph 20a), resulting in one or many of the faults that I have mentioned above.

20a Shuto uke – the buttocks are sticking out, making the stance totally unstable and very stressful for the lower body

KIBA DACHU

The feet should be pointing forwards and the body should be straight from the rear of the shoulder to the hips. The thrust of the body should be forwards and downwards, forcing the feet flat (photograph 21). A good kiba dachu builds power into the knees and hips.

21 Kiba dachu. Note the flat feet and the knees held by muscle groups in the correct positions

Points to avoid

A common mistake is to leave the hips out (see photograph 22), which can hyperextend the lumbar region of the back, causing the kind of 'kissing' spine injury which I discussed in the section on gyaku tzuki. The medial ligaments of the knee are at risk if the feet are turned outwards and the knees are allowed to relax in, as in photograph 22a.

22 Kiba dachu viewed from the side, showing hyperextended lumbar region and buttocks sticking out, which can cause lower back injury

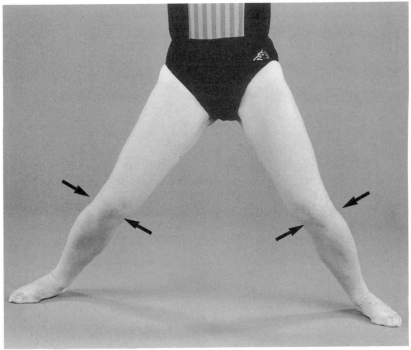

22a Badly executed kiba dachu: the knees have dropped in, allowing the body weight to stretch the inner side of the knee ligaments

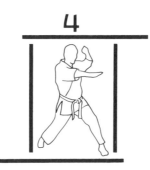

4

BASIC BLOCKS IN A STATIONARY ZENKUTSU DACHU POSITION

(*Note*: I will describe age uke. Although the arm movements are different in the other basic blocks, the movement of the hips, leg and knees will be virtually the same for soto uke, uchi ude uke and gedan barai.)

AGE UKE (hidari)

Adopt a good right-hand gyaku tzuki position. Raise the right hand up, with the fingers pointing upwards and the arm bent at approximately 45 degrees across the body so that the fingers are roughly in line with your left shoulder. With an inhalation of breath, the left hand goes out and forwards, forming an x-type blocking position in line with the chin. At this point the student should be exhaling and rotating the rear knee towards the outside edge of the rear right foot, through 45 degrees of movement, or as near as possible, depending on the flexibility of the hip and ankle. The whole leg should move together, being pushed by the left hip and rotating in a clockwise direction. Both hips should maintain a slight softness, as if just about to sit on a chair. This should prevent the rear knee from locking against the joint.

Try to keep the torso fairly flexed and moving simultaneously with the rear hip and leg with an equal and opposite action to approximately 45 degrees, thus drawing the left arm upwards with the feeling of a punching action and of rolling the elbow and upper arm back towards the head as the wrist rotates through 180 degrees. As the hip and leg twist is executed, the right elbow should be touching the lower ribs and the lower arm is drawn round tightly against the body to maintain stability.

At this point the feet should feel as if they are being forced outwards and the knees should feel as if they are being pushed out by a torsion bar. The right rear hip has a slight give in it, as at the beginning of sitting down. The buttocks and abdomen are locked tight, forcing the body weight forwards and down as if at an angle to the floor, thus transmitting the energy upwards to the arm. If all the muscles are simultaneously locked with the exhalation of breath, the result should be a resounding vibration through the body (as shown in photograph 23). Again, there should be no

23 A correctly performed age uke (upper rising block). Note the body kept inside the line of the foot placement, correct angles of the hips and front blocking arm for maximum efficiency

jarring. To maximise the effect of the block, of course, the shoulders should be pulled down. The elbow should neither be at a 45 degree angle nor protruding too much outside the body, i.e. towards the left-hand side, as this could result in a weakness in the block.

24 Age uke (upper rising block) from the front, badly performed. The rear hips are pulled back too far, allowing the rear leg to straighten and also pulling the front knee to the inside of the stance

Points to avoid

Whilst doing age uke, many people rotate the hip back too far and do not rotate the rear knee. They also have the rear foot at 90 degrees to the front foot. This allows the rear knee to be locked straight and also allows the front knee to be pulled inwards, as photograph 24 shows. This in turn puts excess pressure on the rear knee, because the block (if executed with a partner) puts considerable strain on the ligaments of the rear leg and front leg, and again attacks the medial ligaments of both knees.

If the hip is pulled too far back, in some cases students tense and push the abdomen forwards, which tends to push the front knee out. Also, the elbow tends to be outside the body extremity, as in photograph 25, which destabilises the stance and weakens the

25 Age uke viewed from the front. Bad foot placement, as well as the front knee pushing out too far, and the elbow of the blocking arm outside the body cavity, making the blocking ineffective

block, causing even greater pressure on the rear knee. The coccyx is often drawn up too tightly, resulting in hyperextension of the lumbar region and lower back with the kind of 'kissing' action of the spine already described in the section on gyaku tzuki. This causes a jarring effect in the body. (Often students that practise blocking this way complain of headaches after a training session.) If the elbow is pushed outside the extremity line of the rib cavity, the block is considerably weaker than if it is slightly in towards the centre of the chest.

(*Note*: the same type of body, hip and leg rotation applies to basic blocks or to strikes, such as haito uche or shuto uke, if performed from a gyaku tzuki position in zenkutsu dachu. Obviously, with strikes and straight arm blocks, do prevent the arm from locking at the elbow. Uchi ude uke and soto uke just require the rotation of the elbow and upper arm in synchronisation.)

SOTO UKE

To perform a basic soto uke block in a stationary position, start

26 Soto uke – basic stationary start position

26a Soto uke – half-way stage. Stationary position

26b Soto uke completed. Note the rear knee is rotated in an outward direction at the same time as the elbow is rotated in an inward direction

with a good left zenkutsu dachu, feet hip-width apart, and assume a right gyaku tzuki position, with the right arm outstretched and the fingers open, approximately in line with the sternum. Raise the left hand and arm up so that the index finger is roughly at the height of the top of the left ear, one or two fist distances away from it, as in photograph 26.

With a full inhalation of breath, draw the right arm back so that the elbow touches the hip, but don't move the hip at this point. Simultaneously, allow the left arm to move half way through its rotation, as in photograph 26a. At the same time rotate the rear knee from the downward direction in which it has been facing, through a quarter turn, making sure that the whole leg turns as one unit and leaving a few centimetres of movement behind the knee, so the leg is never jammed straight.

As this rotation occurs, the right hip is pulled smoothly and sharply back. The right elbow is drawn behind the side of the body and the forearm of the left hand is rotated and locked (see photograph 26b). The whole body should be locked simultaneously, especially the inner thigh muscles (adductors), which should cause a vibration throughout the body. This has a beneficial massaging as opposed to a jarring effect on the body.

UCHI UDE UKI
Start from a good left zenkutsu dachu, with the feet hip-width apart and assume a right gyaku tzuki position. Open the left hand, with the fingertips roughly in line with the sternum. The left hand should now be taken across to the right hip bone and with the thumb resting on top, as in photograph 27. At this point, take a full inhalation of breath and then draw the right hand back until the elbow of the right arm touches the right hip and simultaneously move the left arm away from the body, as in photograph 27a.

At this point, exhale sharply, rotating the rear leg in an outward direction, pulling the right hip back and pushing the left hip forwards (the action of the legs is the same as in soto uke, so the same points apply). Draw the right fist back to the right side of the body, tucked in tight. Allow the left arm to move up and complete the block. Care must be taken that the biceps muscle does not contract too early, as this will not give the correct forearm angle to the

27 Uchi uke – basic
stationary start position

27a Half-way stage. Note the hips
have not yet moved. The rear knee
is in a forward-facing direction at
this point

27b Completed uchi
uke. Note the rear knee
is twisted in an outward
direction, as with soto uke

upper arm and will result in a weak block. Aim to form a triangle
with the fist at shoulder height and the elbow not protruding past
the rib cavity (or body line), as in photograph 27b.

GEDAN BARAI

To perform gedan barai from a stationary position, begin by
assuming a good left zenkutsu dachu with the feet hip-width apart.
Adopt a right gyaku tzuki position, with the fist at lower chudan
height. The left hand is now drawn up so the palm of the left fist is
nearly cupping the right ear, as in photograph 28. At this point, a
full inhalation of breath is taken and the right arm is drawn back till
the elbow touches the right hip and simultaneously the left arm is
drawn down towards the mid-section of the body, as in photograph
28a. Then with a sharp exhalation, the right arm is drawn back to
the right side of the body and simultaneously the left forearm is rotated to form the block (see photograph 28b).

As with all the other blocks described earlier, the same rota-

| 28 Gedan barai – basic stationary start position | 28a Gedan barai – half-way stage. The right elbow is drawing back tightly towards the body – the hips have not yet rotated | 28b Gedan barai completed. If all pressures are correct throughout the body, the feet should be flat – the back foot should not be tilted to the inside or outside |

tional movement of the hips and legs is applied. Care should be taken not to allow the elbow to twist up too far. Do not allow the joint to hyperextend as this will result in a similar elbow injury as described in the section on choku tzuki.

Points to note

With all the blocks described above, breathing is an extremely important part of the exercise. Always use a complete inhalation, filling the lower, middle and upper lung completely. Correct, full breathing has a massaging effect on the central organs.

When turning the body to hanmi (half-facing) to execute a block, everyone is slightly different, especially at the beginner stage. The main thing to remember is never push the body into hyperextending the joints, e.g. elbows and knees. Always keep the shoulders down and the back straight, retaining the natural curvature of the spine so that all the muscle groups take a proportion of loading and they all pull in the manner they were designed to do.

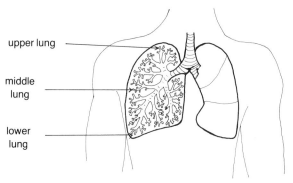

upper lung

middle
lung

lower
lung

Fig. 15 Torso, showing inflation of the lower,
middle and upper lung

No one group of muscles should become overloaded; otherwise, over a long period of time some disfigurement can be caused, especially in children, whose bodies are very susceptible to harm from bad posture.

5

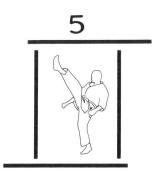

KICKS

MAE GERI (chudan)

This is a snapping kick and should incorporate a whip-like action of the lower leg.

Assume a good zenkutsu dachu, with the hips square on to the front and the arms at the side of the body, roughly in line with the hip. The shoulders should be kept down to maintain tension in the lateral muscles, 'lats', which in turn stabilises the stance (see photograph 29). Keep the hips down to retain the natural curvature of the spine.

29 Zenkutsu dachu – start position for mae geri

30 Mae geri – top of the kick, with the leg just starting to retract. You should 'feel' the inward circle of the kicking knee

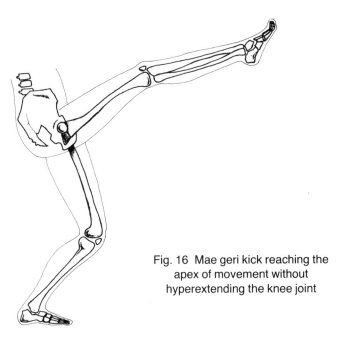

Fig. 16 Mae geri kick reaching the apex of movement without hyperextending the knee joint

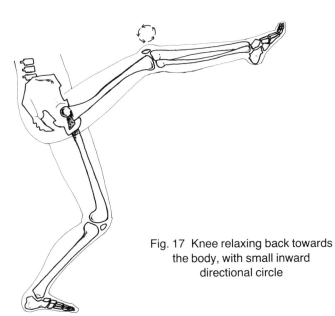

Fig. 17 Knee relaxing back towards the body, with small inward directional circle

Lift the knee up towards the chest and curl the toes back, aiming the foot in a straight line towards the target area. As the lower leg extends, flex the left hip forwards and upwards, pushing in to the kick. This action should be allowed to push the support leg outwards, causing the supporting foot to pivot slightly (as in photograph 30). Do not allow the support knee to straighten. The toes are pulled back and the ankle is flexed just before reaching the target area, pushing the kicking foot forwards. The knee of the kicking leg must not be locked out against the bone. Just at the apex of movement, the rear hip is relaxed and pulled back, which in turn pulls back the kicking leg and hip.

The feeling to aim for is that of the knee making a small inwardly directional circle. If all the various muscle groups are used correctly, the result should be a whip-like action. Throughout the technique, the foot travels in what is virtually a straight line from the ground to the target and back again. It is important to keep the weight over the support leg, both to retain balance and to optimise the recoil action of the kick.

Points to avoid
I have seen many people make the mistake of locking their knee joints out at the apex of the kick (as in photograph 31). Imagine the

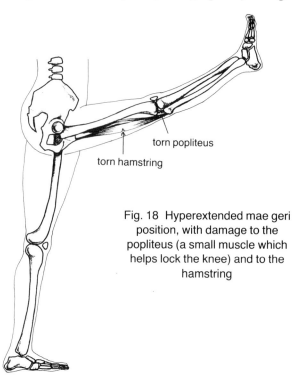

torn popliteus

torn hamstring

Fig. 18 Hyperextended mae geri position, with damage to the popliteus (a small muscle which helps lock the knee) and to the hamstring

31 Mae geri badly executed, with the kicking leg locked at the top of the kick, causing trauma to the joint

effect of the weight of the foot and lower leg being continually rammed against the joint over a few years of training. Sooner or later (sooner, unless the knee is genetically very strong), the knee will start to give problems. The back of the joint capsule may become painfully damaged and the popliteus muscle (responsible for locking the knee out) may become strained. There is also a danger

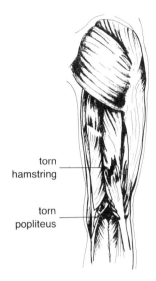

torn
hamstring

torn
popliteus

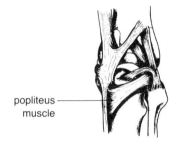

popliteus
muscle

Fig. 20 Back of the right knee, showing
the popliteus muscle in good condition

Fig. 19 Torn hamstring and popliteus
due to faulty technique in mae geri

of tearing the hamstring; an injury which can happen anywhere along the length of the muscle from the tendon attachments at the buttock to the attachments at the knee. If the foot is not pushed forwards at the apex of the kick, the calf muscles and the knee are subject to unnecessary stress. If kicking with a straight leg against a target, the joint tissues could easily tear, because there is no give left in the leg.

In mae geri, the support leg and foot have a great role to play. If the toes are rotated outwards but the support knee is straightened, the whole of the body weight pushes in an unnatural manner against the support knee joint. Most of the stress is taken on the medial ligament (as in photograph 32), causing it to weaken. The medial meniscus could also tear. If, at this point, the support foot were to slip on perspiration on the floor (for example), the knee could actually dislocate. Failure to allow the support leg to swivel can lead to strain and tearing of the cruciates and quadraceps ligaments.

Students who try to kick too high are in danger of tearing muscles and ligaments. Never try to kick a mae geri higher than the height to which you can easily swing up the leg. Another common

32 Mae geri poorly performed with a partner, showing the kicking leg hyperextended and locked, and the rear foot and front knee in an unstable position. This puts tremendous strain on the rear knee joint

cause of ripping is swinging the leg up straight instead of bending the knee first, thus causing the support knee to drop in (see photograph 33).

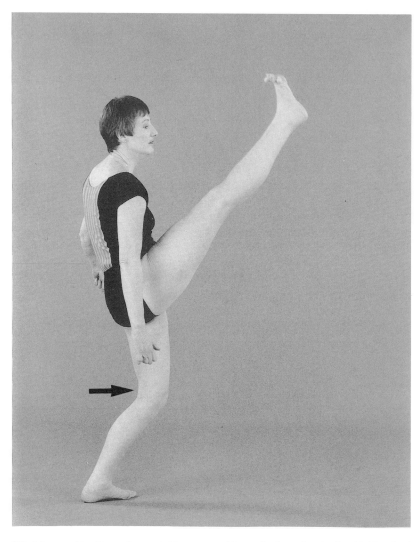

33 Mae geri badly performed. The support knee is dropping in, the kicking foot is in the wrong position and the leg is hyperextended

Incorrect use of the hip can result in hip and lower back problems. In general, if the correlation between the knee and hip action is lost the whole body is jarred.

KEAGE (side snap kick)

When performing this kick from a standing position or when crossing over from a basic kiba dachu position, it is best to start by keeping the body low with the knees bent and the hips soft (the actual height of the stance is determined by the flexibility of the ankle), and keeping the arms out to the side to provide good stability.

For a right side snap kick, keep the left leg bent and the knee flexed out. Do not allow it to relax inwards. Lift the right knee as high as possible towards the underarm and relax the hip, so that the knee points in the direction of travel. The kicking foot should be kept back towards the inner thigh of the support leg. I, like my teacher Kanazawa Sensei, prefer to keep my foot flexed by curling the big toe up and the other four toes down to maintain maximum tension.

34 Keage (side snap kick). Note the support heel twisted round in the direction of the kick

34a Keage – the kicking knee should feel as though it is making an inward circle

Twisting the knee towards the target area like this allows good flexibility of the hip joint and prevents unnecessary forward movement. At this stage, squeeze the left buttock and push the hip forwards and upwards towards the target area. As the hip is raised and the knee and lower leg start to travel outwards, the support foot should be swivelled by the pressure of the quadraceps muscles, so that the heel faces the direction of travel. Tense the right-hand side of the body to keep it as upright as possible (as in photograph 34). At the apex of the kick the left hip should be relaxed and retracted, which in turn pulls back the kicking leg.

Again, imagine the knee making a small upwardly rotating circle back towards the body (as in photograph 34a), so that it never locks out in an unstable position. Once this rotation has taken place, the knee should be drawn back in towards its starting position, whilst the support knee bends to stabilise the stance and retain balance. Of course, the shoulders should be kept down throughout the technique, as this also helps to stabilise the body.

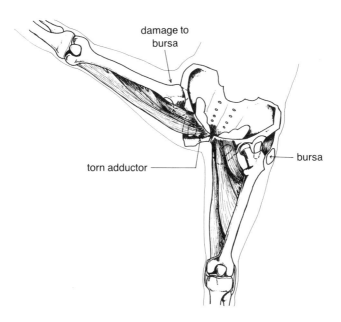

Fig. 21 Faulty keage, showing damage to the adductors (groin strain) and outer hip damage to the bursa

Common faults in keage

For keage, you need good flexibility of the hip and the adductor muscles under it. Many people think that if they get their foot up anyhow above the height of their head that they've done a keage. This kind of faulty technique can seriously damage the hip muscles, leading to groin strain-type injuries and torn adductors. The hip joint itself is particularly at risk here and it is easy to damage the adductors and other soft tissues around the hip, leading to inflam-

35 Keage badly performed. Note the completely unstable support leg, weakening the knee joint (or worse). The kicking leg is too high, so the toes have turned up, and the body is leaning back away from the kick

mation and swelling of the bursa (the fluid sac which protects the joint). The muscles around the supporting hip which act to stabilise the body can be under great strain in a faulty kick.

Another common mistake in keage is to throw the leg out without bending the knee and then to lean back away from the kick (as in photograph 35). This overextension pulls the support knee in and puts dangerous pressure on the inside of it. As you can see from photograph 35, failure to pivot on the foot puts similar pressure on the support knee. This again puts tremendous pressure, as you can see from photograph 35, on the knee's medial ligaments. With all the energy moving forwards, it is quite easy to comprehend the amount of pressure these ligaments are under and how, in this very unstable position, the knee is literally forced sideways in a manner it was never designed to move in.

Note also in photograph 35 the way in which some students, instead of having the foot in a side-on position (sokuto), point the toes up towards the ceiling, or skyward. This turns the technique into a very badly executed mixture of a sideways mae geri/keage. This pointing of the foot is usually an attempt to gain more height and usually indicates lack of flexibility in the adductor muscles of the inner thigh. Look at photograph 35 and imagine the energy travelling forwards towards the target area. Imagine what would happen if there were some moisture on the floor and the support

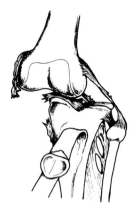

Fig. 22 Left knee, showing dislocation. This can
result from the support leg slipping on
perspiration or from wear and tear

leg slipped backwards as the pressure built up on the knee. In this highly unstable position the leg could partially or fully dislocate, especially if the ligaments have been weakened over a period of time by bad technique. Finally, never try to kick above the height to which you can comfortably swing your leg.

JODAN MAWASHI GERI (snap kick)

Assume a good left zenkutsu dachu position as for mae geri. The body weight should be shifted slightly forward. Bring the right

36a Half-way position for mawashi geri. Note the knee of the kicking leg close to the body

Fig. 23 Hip and leg positioning at the
start of mawashi geri

knee up to the side and as high as possible towards the underarm at
90 degrees to the direction of travel (see photograph 36a). Keep
the heel of the kicking foot tucked in tight towards the buttock.
The right hip and knee can be sent slightly further upwards by flexing the left buttock and pushing up. At the same time, pull the knee
round towards the centre of the body and pivot on the support foot
through 90 degrees. Keep the body upright as much as possible at
this point. Lean slightly forwards if necessary rather than allowing
the body to tilt back (photograph 36b).

The lower part of the leg then goes out towards the target area,
which should be somewhere from the centre to the left-hand side in
line with your body. As with a mae geri, the toes should be pulled
back and the ankle flexed, propelling the foot slightly forwards at
the apex of the kick (as in photograph 36c).

As the foot reaches the apex of the kick, the hips should be relaxing and beginning to move back and the support leg should be bent.
As with other snap kicks, the feeling is as if the knee of the kicking
leg were making a small anti-clockwise circle back towards the
body. This will encourage a whip-like action in the leg and will
enable it to return more easily to a stable position.

Use the quadraceps muscles to keep the knee of the support leg
in its correct structural position at all times. The support leg and

36b Mawashi geri completed. Note that the support foot has twisted. The hips have also twisted, so all the joints are in the correct position

36c Jodan mawashi geri, viewed from the left-hand side. Note the kicking foot in the turned position at the top of the kick

the striking leg should always have a few centimetres of give behind the knees at all times throughout the technique. As the leg returns to its starting position, the support foot swivels back to its original position, ready for the next technique.

Points to avoid

Some people fail to twist properly on the supporting leg, which corkscrews the knee and puts pressure on the lateral and medial ligaments. This sort of movement causes a twisting type of action on the knee, as you can see from photograph 37. This movement done over a period of time can severely weaken the knee.

Another common fault is leaning back away from the kick (as in photograph 38). This can lead to serious back injury by causing the back to flex in the wrong place. The rear of the spine is pinched and the sacreal joint eventually becomes severely strained. Women should be especially careful not to strain the sacreal joint because it can soften and weaken under the influence of hormone changes, e.g. during menstruation.

37 Mawashi geri badly performed. The support foot has not rotated, so the support knee is under twisting pressure

Fig. 24 Knee under tension, showing the effects of 'corkscrewing' in mawashi geri: ligament tears and pinched cartilage on the lateral ligament side

38 Mawashi geri poorly executed: the torso is leaning back and the foot placement is incorrect

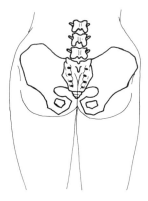

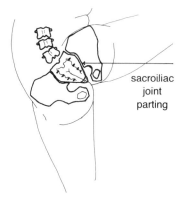

sacroiliac
joint
parting

Fig. 25 The lumbo-sacral
joint is the weakest point in
the vertebral column; it can
be weakened by faulty
technique

Fig. 26 Sacroiliac joint strained
under pressure from a bad kick

Faulty technique can lead to problems around the hip of a similar nature to those outlined in the section on keage: groin strain and tearing of the hamstrings and adductors. Another way I have seen many people do mawashi geri is by stepping across in a sideways fashion, straightening the support knee and virtually swinging the kicking leg up as high as possible, as in photograph 39. If you were to persist in this type of action, hip damage would certainly take place at some stage as the kicks become more powerful and more strain is placed on the hip joint. So, never kick in this fashion beyond the capability of the body, as you are virtually forcing your body into mid-air splits. Locking the knee joint with bone against bone is an injurious fault common to all kicking techniques. Avoid this at all costs.

In karate we use very fast ballistic movement. Ballistic stretching (stretching that forces the muscle length by jerky movement) causes the 'stretch reflex' to occur, which actually shortens and tightens the muscles. Static stretching overcomes this and promotes a more permanent increase in muscle length, thus allowing ballistic movements to take place without overstretching the muscles. So, looking at the way I have described the way not to kick in the last section, it is easy to appreciate the amount of strain

39 Badly performed mawashi geri – the leg has swung up,
which could cause tearing to the adductors and injury to the
sacroiliac joint

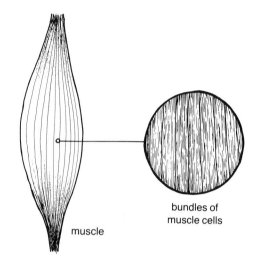

muscle

bundles of
muscle cells

Fig. 27 Composition of muscles

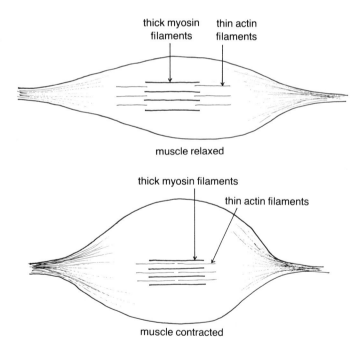

thick myosin
filaments

thin actin
filaments

muscle relaxed

thick myosin filaments

thin actin filaments

muscle contracted

Fig. 28 Thin filaments sliding between thick filaments, thus
causing muscle contraction

put on the muscles, especially the adductors. If a karateka forces the kick higher than the body capability, the effects will be exactly the same, so no wonder many people finish a training session and find they are as stiff as a board the following day.

KEKOMI (side thrust kick)

Begin by assuming a basic kiba dachu position and stepping across. If performing a kick on the right-hand side, the right hand should be kept down and taut behind the leg as the kick is performed (a gedan barai position) and the left hand should be in a fist against the hip.

In a basic kekomi, the support leg should be kept bent. Bring the knee of the kicking leg up at about 45 degrees to the direction of travel. Keep this knee back, and don't allow it to lift the hip of that side up and out. Keep the hip back as if about to sit in a chair and maintain tension in the upper body, especially in the 'lats' of the kicking side.

As the kicking leg starts to extend towards the target area, try to maintain the upper body position by squeezing slightly harder with the arm of the kicking side. Then rotate the hips over sharply, simultaneously pivoting on the foot of the supporting leg so that the heel of the support foot is pointing in the same direction of travel as the kick. (I share the opinion with my teacher Kanazawa Sensei that the foot should have the big toe up and the small toes curled under, as mentioned earlier with keage. The foot should also be slightly angled, rather than at 90 degrees to the leg, as this will help lock the muscles and give greater tension to the foot.)

As the hips roll and the support heel twists, the foot is thrust out and the leg rolls from the rotation of the hips. Tighten the buttocks as hard as possible and maintain a strong feeling of kimae in the stomach and lower abdomen. The twisting action of the hips and the pulling action of the abdomen should then set up a chain reaction of muscles contracting in the hamstring, thigh and calf. It should be possible to thrust the leg straight without going against the joint of the knee (see photograph 40).

If the muscles are used in this way it should produce a thrust with a slight rotational feeling within the muscles and leg, much like the twisting rotational action of the choku tzuki. This also helps the

40 Kekomi geri (side thrust kick). Note the tension in the kicking leg so that it is not jammed hard in a hyperextended position against the knee joint

muscles to lock without unnecessary strain being placed upon them. If there is no twisting action, the muscles don't lock as easily and are strained.

At the completion of the kick, the whole technique should have a slight 'banana' shape from heel to shoulder (as in photograph 41), with the hips slightly more pronounced than the heel and shoulder

41 Kekomi viewed from the side, showing clearly the leg in a straight position, but with tension in the hips. This helps bow the body and the leg to avoid placing pressure on the back of the kicking knee

line. If you aim to produce the feeling of twisting the heel over and upwards above the height of the toes towards the ceiling, this should help the locking action and prevent the knee from jarring itself back as far as it can go against the joint. As with most of the techniques, this does take quite a while to perfect.

When executing a traditional technique there are many things to think about if it is to be executed with power, speed and focus and without damaging any of the joints in the process. If the technique feels odd to start with, it is a matter of persevering slowly and cautiously at lower levels whilst practising the chain reaction of muscles and tension. It is advisable to kick slowly, checking the technique all the way through and ending up with a nicely executed technique at knee height. It is much more advantageous to do a technique properly at a lower level than to try to kick too high before the technique is sufficiently well understood. This avoids unnecessary strain on the body. There should be a few centimetres of 'give' behind the knee of the kicking leg after the kick has been executed if you have locked the muscle groups correctly.

Points to avoid

As you raise the knee of your kicking leg, the kicking foot is brought forwards as well and the kicking hip is allowed to move in

Fig. 29 Bad kekomi, causing torn adductors

an upward fashion, which causes tension in the buttocks and a general straightening of the support leg. As the kick is performed there is no rotation of the hip to support the knee of the kicking leg (see photograph 42). If the support foot is not rotated, there is a twisting, jarring action focused on the support knee. This puts undue pressure on the cartilage of the kicking knee and there is a

42 Bad kekomi geri. Note that the hips have not been rotated to give muscular support to the legs

compounding hammering effect on the knee joint which could lead to the onset of arthritis, etc.

Photograph 43 shows the lack of rotation of the hips to support the kicking knee and the failure to pivot the support foot, which places the whole body in a very unnatural and dangerous position.

43 The support foot has not been rotated, so the hips are in an incorrect position. This will have a detrimental effect on all the lower joints, especially if striking a kickbag

44   Well-executed kekomi, viewed from the back. There is a slight bend
in the support leg, with the foot rotated towards the kicking direction.
The hips are used to lock the kicking legs, so that a few centimetres of
movement remain behind the kicking knee joint

Photograph 44, illustrates the correct technique. You can see: the
hip rotation; the support leg still has plenty of 'give' in the correct
fashion; and the support foot has been rotated. This gives extremely good support to the kicking leg, as all the muscles of the

body can be simultaneously locked and the joints remain within their range of movements. So, even if you were striking at a kicking bag the joints would not be forced into an unnatural position by the pressure of contact, as they would be by anyone imitating the technique shown in photograph 43.

Correct body positioning is very important in kekomi. If the body is incorrectly positioned, the hamstring could be stretched and torn. The popliteus muscle behind the knee is also at risk if the kicking leg is forced straight. In the support leg, the medial ligaments and meniscus (medial cartilage) are vulnerable if the foot is not pivoted correctly and the knee is not kept slightly bent.

6

MOVEMENT

Many problems in movement stem from leaving the front foot out. This overstrains the knee joint, causing it to rock back. It also leads to the rear knee being jammed straight because too much pressure is being put on it. Another common fault occurs when a student blocks too near the centre of the body and overbends the blocking arm.

OI TZUKI

The action of moving forwards in zenkutsu dachu is basically the same for oi tzuki, age uke, soto uke, gedan barai, etc. Only the arm movements differ. I have chosen oi tzuki as our example here. The arm action will not be described in detail, as it is the same as for choku tzuki.

When moving forwards in zenkutsu dachu, you have to re-member a number of important points. A fraction before moving off from a left-hand gedan barai postion (as in photograph 45), you should slightly relax the rear knee and hip. This preloads the muscles of the rear leg. (It is an extremely subtle movement, and can be compared with jumping when you sink before springing up in order to make more height.) Then move forwards by flexing the muscles of the rear leg, relaxing the front (left) knee and allowing the left hip to move forwards, transferring the body weight over the left leg (the left foot should not have moved, as in photograph 45a).

The hips should be soft at this stage, as if about to squat or sit back in a chair. Draw the right foot up towards the left. As the right foot reaches the three-quarter stage and becomes the front foot, the left leg (now the rear leg – see photograph 45b) can simply be pushed out, rotating the knee outwards, because the front leg is moving

45 Left (hidari) gedan barai, ready
for forward basic movement of
oi tzuki

45a Half-way through oi tzuki.
Note the feet drawn together, and
the relaxed hips and knees

out also to a hip-width position for stability. If you apply pressure
to the quadraceps muscles, this will push the knee and leg, and
rotate it in more of an outward direction (but only slightly). Simultaneously, lock the buttocks, abdomen and inner thigh muscles
(adductors) a fraction before the punch is delivered, sending a
shock-like wave through the body to the fist, with the muscles of
the hip and thigh taking up the shock of the abrupt stopping action
of the movement (see photograph 45c). The hip should be kept at
the same height throughout this technique, whether the movement

45b Three-quarter stage. At this point the muscle groups of the left leg (rear leg) are being pre-loaded automatically to push the body forwards

45c Fully executed oi tzuki. Note the rear support leg has twisted out slightly at an angle, thereby stabilising the whole stance on impact

is forward or back. The arm movements of the punch are the same as for choku tzuki, and the same mistakes should be avoided.

Points to avoid

With basic movements in zenkutsu dachu, make sure that the rear foot is not sticking out at 90 degrees to the front foot. Ensure that the rear leg is not jammed solid against the joint, as this tends to lock the rear hip, putting tremendous pressure on the inside of the

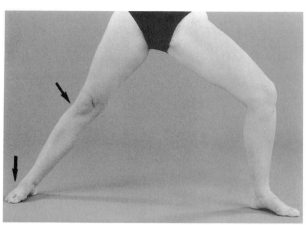

46 Zenkutsu dachu – the rear foot is at the wrong angle and the rear leg is too straight

47 Incorrect start position for basic oi tzuki. The front foot is turned out at the wrong angle

47a Start of a bad oi tzuki. The knee is being forced inwards through bad front foot placement

rear knee (as in photograph 46). Many people move the front foot out 20 or 30 degrees as movement starts to take place (see photograph 47). If this happens, the front knee becomes very unstable. As the weight is transferred over to the left leg it then has a detrimental twisting action on the knee and stretches the medial ligaments (as in photograph 47a). As the pressure builds up, this could cause the kneecap (patella) to be pulled across the knee joint in an uneven manner, which causes uneven loading of the joint surfaces. As the three-quarter stage is reached, the knee is in such a

47b Half-way stage of a bad oi tzuki. Note the foot already sticking out to the side

47c Three-quarter stage. Through incorrect posture and positioning, there is no proper pre-loading of the muscles for this technique to be executed properly

destabilised position that if the foot should slip in any moisture on the dojo floor it could cause the knee to dislocate (I have seen this happen).

After the three-quarter stage (see photographs 47b and 47c), if the leg is rotated and the hip is locked, moving the right hip slightly forwards will probably result in a slight body lean, with the hips dead square. This will force the back leg to be ground against the joint, causing strain of the medial ligaments, as photographs 48 and 48a show. Photograph 48a also clearly illustrates an unstable oi tzuki, as the rear foot is turned out at 90 degrees to the front foot. Also, the front foot is not in line. Therefore, in this position the kneecap (patella) is drawn hard back against the knee joint; the deeper the stance, the greater this pressure becomes, particularly with the abrupt stopping action of an oi tzuki.

Because the leg is now straight and the body's natural movement is to have a slight angle forward from the torso, there is a tendency

48 Badly performed oi tzuki. Poor foot placement of the rear foot, which means that the rear leg is too straight, puts medial ligaments on the inside of the knee under great strain

48a Bad oi tzuki viewed from the front. Note the bad foot placement, making the stance very unstable on completion of the technique

Fig. 30 Inside of a normal, fissured and fractured patella (deep stances can cause the front kneecap to pull back and grind across the top of the joint)

to squeeze the lower back too hard in an effort to straighten the upper body. This puts unnecessary tension on the lumbar region of the spine, causing a 'kissing' action of the spinal vertebrae, as described in the section on gyaku tzuki.

I do not recommend the very deep stances which are adopted by some Shotokan stylists. In a very deep stance the front kneecap is pulled back and ground across the top of the knee joint, causing fissuring, wear and stress. The ligaments and muscles have to work across a larger area, resulting in a lot of unnecessary strain. If the front foot is turned out as movement takes place, there is a torsion effect inside the knee and the kneecap is pulled back at an uneven angle. Under the considerable forces produced by moving in oi tzuki, this can result in uneven wear on the patella and strain on the medial ligament.

MOVING IN BACK STANCE

When moving forwards in back stance, transfer the weight forwards by bending the front knee and move the rear leg (in this case the right leg) up parallel to the left, but maintain 90% of the weight on the left leg. As the right leg reaches the three-quarter stage, the back leg (now the left leg) should be pivoted on the ball of the foot as the front foot continues in a straight line of travel. The rear knee must be kept stable and the quadraceps pushed back as the left foot is pivoted, so that on completion the front foot is in a straight line and the rear foot is at 90 degrees to it. The hips should be at a forty-five degree angle. The stance should be completed as described on page 52 (back stance).

If, however, the karateka finds difficulty in stabilising the stance, the front leg can be moved slightly wide of the centre line to make the stance more stable, especially in the early stages of training.

It is important not to move so quickly that the body weight is pushed too far forwards into a zenkutsu dachu front stance and then rocked back into back stance, as this has an unbalancing effect on the movement, as described in 'Points to avoid' on pages 57-8.

7

SELECTED MOVES FROM KATA

In teaching around the country over the years and talking to students, certain techniques have emerged as being particularly problematic and potentially dangerous. In this chapter I will look at a few of these moves taken from the Heian katas and Tekki Shodan.

HEIAN SHODAN

This is a basic kata, so most of the points concerning zenkutsu dachu, oi tzuki, age uke, etc. have already been covered in other parts of this book. Once you have learned the basic movements and form of the kata, bearing the technical points in mind, it should always be enjoyable. You will experience new feelings from correct body movements and will exert greater control over these movements. This in turn will ensure that every training session is a new experience; lessons should never become boring or mundane.

HEIAN NIDAN

This kata is much more flowing than Heian Shodan, with various stance changes but basically a lot of back stance. I have already covered back stance, keage, zenkutsu dachu, etc. in previous chapters; the same points apply.

Half-way through the kata, after the last hidari shuto uke (see photograph 49), there is a haito (ridge hand) uke (see photograph 49a). Many students throw their arm back behind their body at the same time as moving the left leg out to the left into a zenkutsu dachu. If performed fast, this movement can tear the pectoral muscles and damage the anterior joint capsule. It is a potentially

49 Hidari shuto uke (knife-hand block in back stance) prior to haito uke in Heian Nidan

49a Start of haito uke in Neian Nidan. The right arm is not hyperextended, but is in line with the rear leg

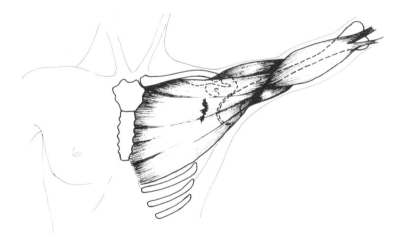

Fig. 31 Torn pectoral muscle as a result of hyperextension when throwing the arm back with a violent action

dislocating position for the shoulder, so great care must be taken not to overextend it.

The karateka is also starting to move the hips in a slightly different manner whilst kicking mae geri. The hip of the kicking leg begins to be used whilst in a slightly forward position of the support hip (see photograph 50), as a gyaku tzuki is to be performed after the mae geri. The basic principles of mae geri should still be adhered to and the support leg hip especially must not be frozen and drawn forward (see section on how *not* to do a mae geri), since

50 Uchi uke in Heian Nidan. Note the right hip pushed forwards in gyaku hanmi (reverse half-facing)

51 Mae geri. The body is in a good stable position and the hands are correctly placed ready for the next technique

this could cause the knee to have problems in the future. Care should be taken that the inside muscles of the support leg are kept under tension, as with the basic mae geri, and that the hips and legs are moved as in the basic move explained earlier in the book (see photograph 51).

HEIAN SANDAN – fumikomi geri

We will look at the first fumikomi geri landing in kiba dachu with the first migi empi uki and uraken. Many students do this movement as a mikuzuki block and swing the leg out to the right, wide of the body, and then up fairly straight, often leaning backwards and taking the centre of gravity forward from the rear leg (left leg). This places tremendous strain on the knee and quite often on the lower back, especially if the student is fairly tight in the inner thigh muscles (adductors). The leg is brought down in a stamping fashion with most of the body weight behind it. As a lot of dojos have fairly solid floors without too much 'give', this can cause stress fractures and bruising to the fatty pad of the heel – an injury which takes a particularly long time to heal. It can also cause anterior shin pain in the front of the leg.

Fig. 32 Particularly bad fumikomi geri technique can cause fracture to the heel

If you perform the movement as a fumikomi geri, as originally intended, the knees remain bent in both the supporting and the striking legs and, as the striking leg is taken across the body, you can simultaneously pivot on the support foot, keeping the support knee pressed back in its correct position for the joint (as shown in photographs 52-52b). The striking leg can then do a small inward rotation quite swiftly as if slicing down to the floor, and can be slid to a stop as in photograph 53, rather than the heel being stamped into the ground. This prevents jarring occurring in the body, and

52 Heian Sandan. Fumikomi geri at the apex of the movement. The kick does not necessarily have to be as high as this, but the knees should remain bent at all times

52a Fumikomi starting to descend. The
support knee must not be allowed to drop in
during this movement

52b Fumikomi nearing completion. The right
hip is held back, ready to move forwards
to lock the stance

53 The author emphasising the completion of fumikomi. Note the
foot starting to slide into the floor rather than the heel
being slammed down

there is also no recoil shock, which must be avoided because it injures not only the joints but the spine itself.

Once you have arrived in kiba dachu from the first fumikomi, with a migi empi uke, do not then drive the arm out so straight when performing the uraken uchi that the elbow is hyperextended (see photograph 54) – as is seen so often when watching this kata performed by many Shotokan stylists. If hyperextension occurs in the elbow joint it will cause the same problems as those associated with choku tzuki (see pp. 36-40). If you concentrate on tensing as the fist rotates, the biceps should come into play to lock the arm by means of the muscle system before it has reached the hyperextension state (see photograph 54a).

If a child's elbow is misused and damaged in this way over a long period of time the result could be a defect in the function of that joint or even disfigurement.

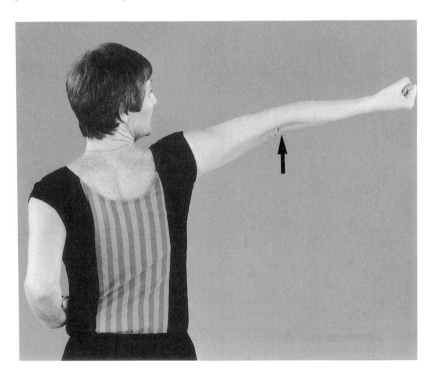

54 Badly performed uraken with hyperextended elbow

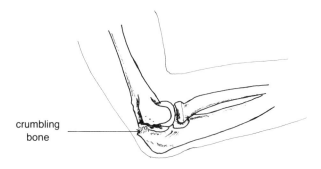

crumbling
bone

Fig. 33 An ulna crumbling against the radius;
to avoid this, do not overextend the elbow joint
in uraken uchi in Heian Sandan

54a Uraken performed properly. Note that there is still plenty of movement
left in the elbow joint

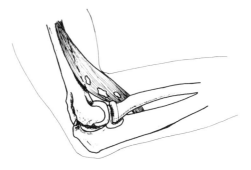

Fig. 34 Build-up of bony matter in soft tissue; this problem
is associated with poor arm techniques

HEIAN YONDAN

Heian Yondan has many back stances and kicks, such as mae geri,
keage and hiza geri. It also has uraken, which I have discussed in
the section on Heian Sandan. Care should be taken at the shuto
gedan barai and at the jodan migi shuto uchi (see photographs 55
and 56), as the elbow joint can easily be hyperextended (see photo-

55 Shuto gedan barai in Heian
Yondan correctly performed

56 Jodan migi shuto uchi in Heian
Yondan correctly performed

graphs 57 and 58), resulting in the same injury to the elbow joint as previously described when discussing choku tzuki (see pp. 36-40). It is especially important for women, who, like children, have a more supple joint system than men, not to be so enthusiastic whilst performing a kata that they forget the basic principles of how the joints function.

57 Badly performed gedan shuto. Note the hyperextended elbow joint

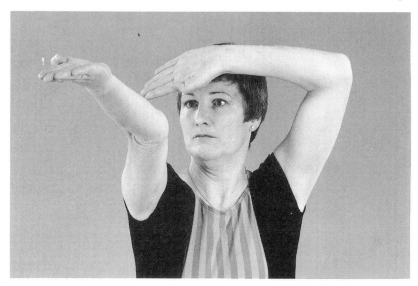

58 Poorly executed jodan shuto uchi. Note the excessively hyperextended elbow joint

HEIAN GODAN

We have been through most of the basic positions of arm, knee and leg joints earlier in the book. If you take care to observe the basic movements correctly, when performing this kata there are no exceptionally injurious techniques that have not already been covered.

The jump is not especially injurious, because the give in the knees will absorb most of the shock on landing (as in photographs 59, 60a and 60b), but the student should take care not to land, as many still do, banging the knee onto the ground. This will cause trauma to the kneecap and its smooth joint surface. Landing too

Fig. 35 Fractured patella as a result of landing too forcibly in Heian Godan

59 Koho tzuki age in reino-ji dachu (ready position for jump in Heian Godan)

60a   The jump in Heian Godan. The legs are tucked up in a correct position for landing

60b Heian Godan – correct landing position in kosa dachu, gedan juji uke

61 Bad landing in Heian Godan, which can result in serious
injury to the knee joint

heavily could even fracture the kneecap. The correct position is shown in photograph 61, where you can clearly see both legs acting as shock absorbers on landing.

TEKKI SHODAN

The most injurious technique in Tekki Shodan, and one that I have seen many students over the years doing badly, is the technique namiashi. I think some people believe that the knee joint is a ball

62 Author performing namiashi geri in Tekki Shodan. Note that the kicking side hip is relaxed back, allowing rotation of the kicking leg

joint and can rotate in front of them somewhat like a hip ball joint. It is of course a hinge joint. The only reason it can move to the side and perform the technique namiashi is because of the rotating action of the hip (see photograph 62).

The knee has a very limited sideways movement. If a student in kiba dachu does not use the hips properly, as is the case, but merely lifts the foot towards the groin or towards the centre of the body, this action puts tremendous strain on the joint of the striking leg. It also pulls in the inner thigh muscles and puts great strain on the knee joint of the support leg. The lateral ligament of the kicking leg and the medial ligament of the support leg take most of the strain.

There is also the possibility of damage to the hip joint. The height to which the foot can be drawn up towards the body area is solely dependent on the flexibility of the hip joint, particularly the hamstring muscle. The movement should be performed, if you are in a kiba dachu doing Tekki Shodan, by slightly altering the angle of the hips and slightly pushing back and lowering the kicking side hip. You should then simultaneously push into the support leg and allow your body to lean slightly towards the side of the kick. Your hips should be slightly turned and somewhat lowered. The pressure should be forced back into the supporting leg while the opposite leg is off the ground.

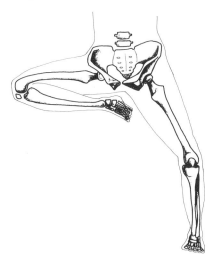

Fig. 36 Skelatal drawing of namiashi geri in Tekki Shodan

At this stage, the foot can be drawn up towards the groin whilst simultaneously rotating the upper thigh of the kicking side to the maximum of its rotation. This means that the knee is pointing down towards the floor and the foot is higher than the knee, if possible, but the knee joint is moving in the manner for which it is designed, i.e. it is a hinge joint (see photographs 63, 63a and 63b).

63 Start of namiashi geri in Tekki Shodan. The kicking leg is already turned out to allow the foot to 'flow' upwards

From this group of photographs you can see fairly clearly the way the kicking leg should be brought up to avoid tearing the medial ligaments of the knee or putting undue strain on any other parts of the supporting knee or hip joints. If you are quite supple, the knee can be raised up parallel to the floor, with the foot on the same level or a fraction higher, as you would do if sitting in a lotus

63a Half-way. Note that the right knee joint is in the natural position

or half-lotus position. It is easy to practise this type of movement by standing in a kiba dachu 90 degrees to a wall, with your right arm (for a migi namiashi) resting against the wall so that it can be used as a prop when you slowly lift and rotate your right leg. If you are fairly tight in the hips, you should perform this slowly and see how far you can rotate your hip and lift the foot to determine the height

63b Complete namiashi geri, without the knee joint
being strained

to which you should be applying this technique during kata. For example, if you can only lift and drop the knee in line with the supporting leg knee, then this is the height to which you should perform namiashi during kata. If you practise the technique carefully and correctly, you will find that this will in time improve it and it will naturally gain more height. On the other hand, if you just use force to try to gain more height, it will invariably weaken the knee joint and tendons, and could lead to a dangerous scenario in the future.

8

PRACTISING WITH A PARTNER

Whilst travelling around the UK and elsewhere, I often observe students who are doing basic kumite. In gohon (five-step kumite) and kihon (basic one-step), the defender should block age uke, for example, as in photograph 64. He should then flex and twist the

64 Age uke at the end of gohon kumite

hip, punching gyaku tzuki with full power but, as he is close to his partner, should keep the elbow of the punching arm bent to control the distance. The karateka can build up speed, power and excellent control by stopping the punch in this fashion. Also, the rest of the body has been used correctly, as you can see from photograph 64a.

64a Correct counter gyaku tzuki using whole body movement. Note how the force of impact is controlled by bending the elbow

Many karateka, however, seem to think that after the block it is a good idea to punch the partner in the stomach or the sternum with the gyaku tzuki. In order to do this, they straighten the punching arm and strike, but do not use the hips and lower body in unison, as in photograph 65. This is not a good way for the defender to use his

65 Badly performed gyaku tzuki, with restricted use of the hips and contacting with a straight-armed fist

66 Badly performed gyaku tzuki, especially for the partner!

body and is certainly very dangerous for the attacker. If, as in our mock-up photograph 66, you were to execute the technique properly, the punch would drive the attacker back or would literally break his bones.

Whilst doing kumite, the attacker, working with an equal grade who has been well drilled in the techniques, should attack with great force so that the defender can really test his defence against the attack. When counter-attacking, however, it is very dangerous for the defender to slam kicks and punches into the body of his partner. As karateka, we should be helping each other to advance, and should be very careful not to injure our partners in training. This applies very much to children who have immature bodies.

9

BREATHING

Most karateka whom I have observed do not seem to understand fully the importance of breathing correctly. It is very important to be able to control the full inhalation and exhalation of breath while performing various techniques, so that your body can maintain its strength, and the mind, its clarity.

Take, for example, a basic oi tzuki (lunge punch) starting from a left gedan barai (downward block) as in photograph 28b, page 69. Whilst moving the right leg up to the left leg, the karateka should simultaneously be making a full inhalation, using the lower, middle and upper lung. This should produce a feeling of swelling the stomach, then the rib cavity and then the upper chest – in that order. Once the right leg has passed the left leg, as in photograph 45b, page 101, from that point the karateka should simultaneously force the breath out and complete the movement of oi tzuki, as in photograph 45c, page 101. This is achieved by tensing the stomach muscles, but not by concaving the chest. In fact, quite the opposite should happen: the chest should be pushed forwards as the stomach muscles are tensed. The feeling is as if someone is compressing the lung area from the back to produce a forceful bellows-like effect.

Of course, the body is completely tense at the focal point of the punch. At the conclusion of the punch, after the rush of air from the body, the breath can be shut off sharply by pushing the tongue against the back of the teeth. This takes some practice, but it can soon be achieved.

From controlling the breath in this manner, you can then go on to controlling it in combinations. If we look at sambon tzuki (three consecutive punches) as our example, the same format of movement as oi tzuki is followed, but breathing changes to allow only half the breath out on the first punch. As you complete the first oi tzuki, the breath is shut off sharply and you maintain the other half in your lungs. After a slight pause the next two punches can be delivered using the remaining breath in the same way: split the breath in two with two sharp exhalations at the focusing of the punches.

You can adjust your breath and experiment with the effects. Using sambon tzuki again as an example, you may wish to split your breath into three, with an equal amount of exhalation on each breath.

When using basic combination techniques, such as age uke, gyaku tzuki, it is extremely important to control the breath, slitting it into two so that there is an equal amount of energy both to produce the block and also to produce a forceful exhalation for the counter.

Breathing control should be taught with every technique from the very beginning, so that the karateka can learn internal control over the breath in the lungs at the same time as learning each movement.

RE-CENTRING THE BREATH

After doing combination work or kata, many karateka end the sequence tired and out of breath. They bow to the sensei, they double over to try to snatch a few breaths and then the sensei shouts the next command and the karateka start moving again. At this stage their bodies are often too deprived of oxygen to function correctly. Injuries can soon follow as concentration levels start to wane rapidly.

In Jin Sei Kai students are taught to return to yoi after a series of movements or kata. Whilst drawing into a yoi position, they make a full inhalation using the lower, middle and upper lungs, swelling the stomach and filling the rib cavity and the chest with a fully complete inhalation. In a relaxed fashion and with the minimum of tension, they then squeeze the air out of the body by drawing the hands and arms slightly together in the yoi position. The stomach is being drawn in and up at this stage, with a feeling of pushing the navel back inside the body as far as possible. The breath should now be fully exhaled and there should be a feeling of a hollow in the stomach and abdominal region. The diaphragm is being pushed up, compressing the upper organs, and the spine will be slightly rounded at completion. Students then straighten the spine and inhale, dropping the diaphragm, with a feeling of swelling the stomach area, ribs and chest with oxygen. At the same time they push down, with the fingers pointing forwards and the arms straight, as if pushing down on two gate posts. Then the whole body is just relaxed with an exhalation, and returned to the yoi position, whereupon the karateka will bow to finish the kata or sequence.

This system is used after every series of movements, as it ensures that karateka can reoxygenate themselves after a period of intense activity. With the combination of correct control over the breath whilst doing the various tasks and techniques, and breathing correctly at the end, they are also guaranteeing a massaging effect on the vital organs. Over the years we have had great success with this type of breathing in helping people with nervous complaints or breathing problems, especially asthma.

CONCLUSION

Karate, in my opinion, is one of the best ways to keep mind, body and spirit in healthy condition. As modern science unfolds, we learn more and more about the intimate side of ourselves and the way muscles perform best, the relationship between body and mind and the various calming effects that certain movements can have on the mind as far as stress, etc. is concerned. If you analyse the finer points of karate movement, you will find many modern theories of muscle movement put into practice to a large degree, albeit sometimes in a little obscure way.

In this book I have not, unfortunately, been able to give the amount of pressure that is put upon the joints of the body or the pressures that the tendons and ligaments have to withstand during various techniques. The pressures are considerable and to obtain this information involves complex scientific techniques; most people would perhaps find the information too technical, anyway. What the karateka and karate instructor must remember is that if a technique or movement within that technique is done badly or injuriously over a number of years, the pressures are such that in most cases some form of injury or irritation will occur. This will have an adverse effect on that person's lifestyle, and is particularly the case with children, whose bodies are still immature. We should be trying to make karate enhance our lives so that we can remain fit until we die. It would be a shame to spend the last five or ten years of life with a loss of mobility due to misunderstandings of body movement whilst training in earlier life, so please think about the joints in your body and remember that they can all wear out.

If anyone feels that they would like more information about a certain area of their training they can always contact me through the Jin Sei Kai General Secretary, Mr M Gorman, 2B Green Lane, St Albans, Herts AL3 6HA or through the Jin Sei Kai Administrator, Mrs W. Russell, 29 Gallows Hill, Kings Langley, Herts WD4 8PG.

INDEX